From ....

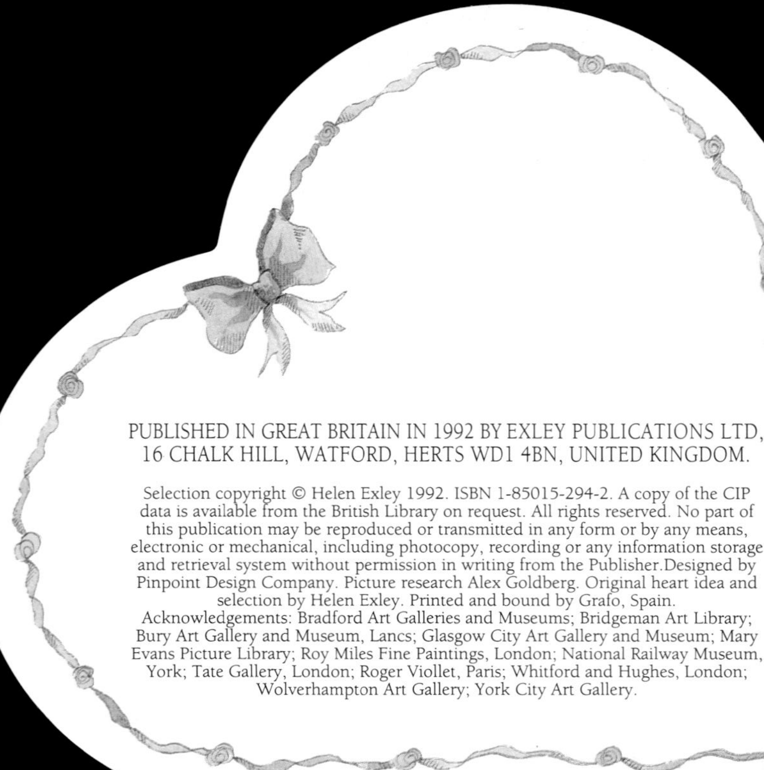

PUBLISHED IN GREAT BRITAIN IN 1992 BY EXLEY PUBLICATIONS LTD,
16 CHALK HILL, WATFORD, HERTS WD1 4BN, UNITED KINGDOM.

 ISBN 1-85015-294-2. A copy of the CIP data is available from the British Library on request. Designed by Pinpoint Design Company. Picture research Alex Goldberg. Original heart idea and selection by Helen Exley. Printed and bound by Grafo, Spain.
Acknowledgements: Bradford Art Galleries and Museums; Bridgeman Art Library; Bury Art Gallery and Museum, Lancs; Glasgow City Art Gallery and Museum; Mary Evans Picture Library; Roy Miles Fine Paintings, London; National Railway Museum, York; Tate Gallery, London; Roger Viollet, Paris; Whitford and Hughes, London; Wolverhampton Art Gallery; York City Art Gallery.

Thoughts
-OF-
Love
Edited by Helen Exley

Love is an act of endless forgiveness, a tender look which becomes a habit.

≈

PETER USTINOV
b.1921

Love, as told by
the seers of old,
Comes as a butterfly
tipped with gold.
Flutters and flies in sunlit skies,
Weaving round hearts that were
one time cold.

≈

ALGERNON CHARLES SWINBURNE
(1837-1909)

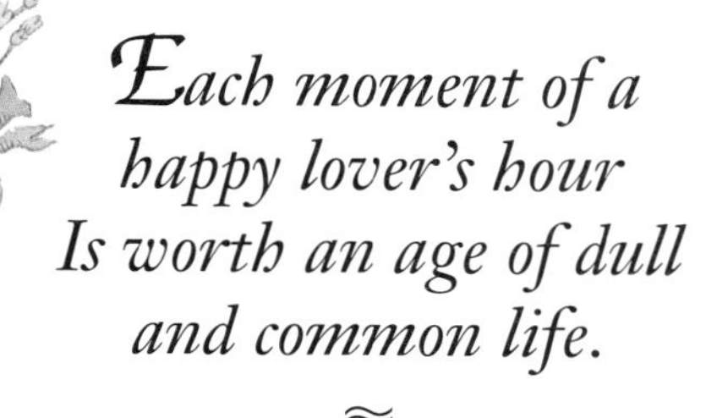

Each moment of a
happy lover's hour
Is worth an age of dull
and common life.

≈

APHRA BEHN
(1640-1689)
from "Younger Brother"

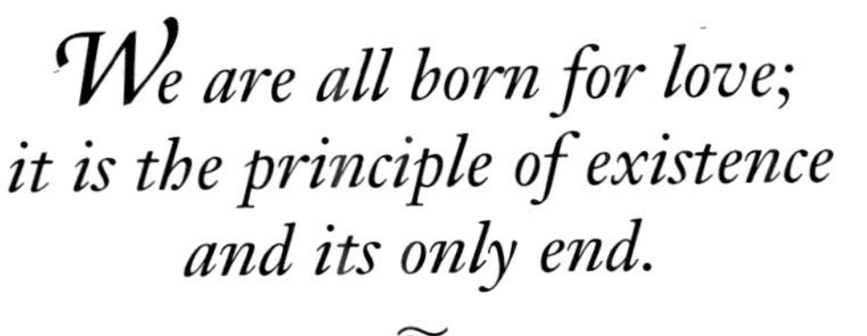

We are all born for love;
it is the principle of existence
and its only end.

≈

BENJAMIN DISRAELI
(1804-1881)
from "Sibyl"

The supreme happiness
of life is the conviction
that we are loved.
≈
VICTOR HUGO
(1802-1885)

To be a lover is not to make love, but to find a new way to live.

≈

PAUL LA COUR

...And when Love
speaks, the voice of all the gods
Makes heaven drowsy with the harmony.
Never durst poet touch a pen to write
Until his ink were temper'd with
Love's sighs.
≈
WILLIAM SHAKESPEARE

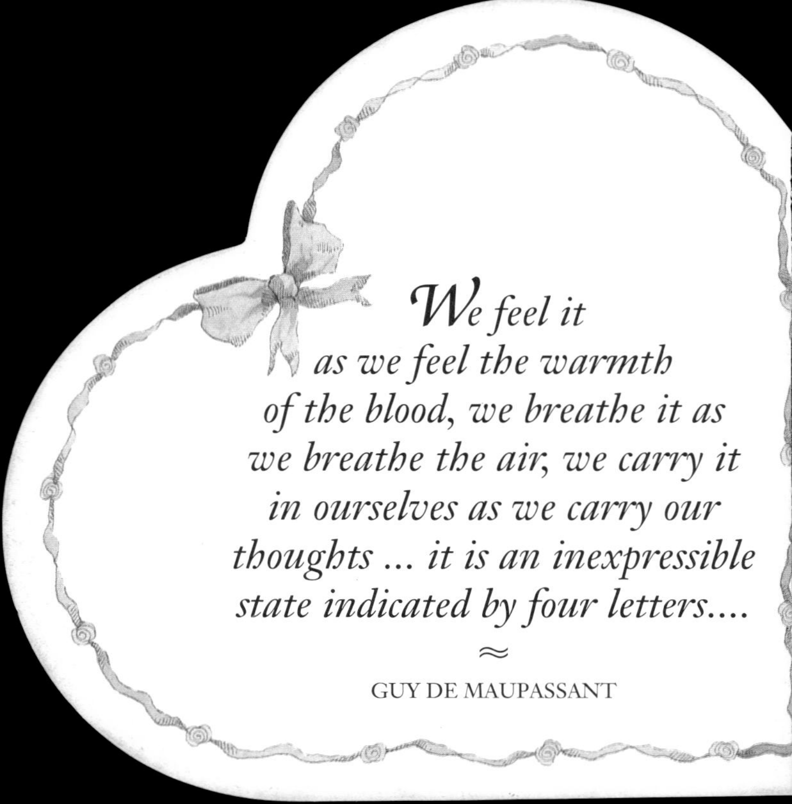
We feel it
as we feel the warmth
of the blood, we breathe it as
we breathe the air, we carry it
in ourselves as we carry our
thoughts ... it is an inexpressible
state indicated by four letters....
≈
GUY DE MAUPASSANT

For one human being to love another: that is perhaps the most difficult of all our tasks, the ultimate, the last test and proof, the work for which all other work is but preparation.

≈

RAINER MARIA RILKE
(1875-1926)

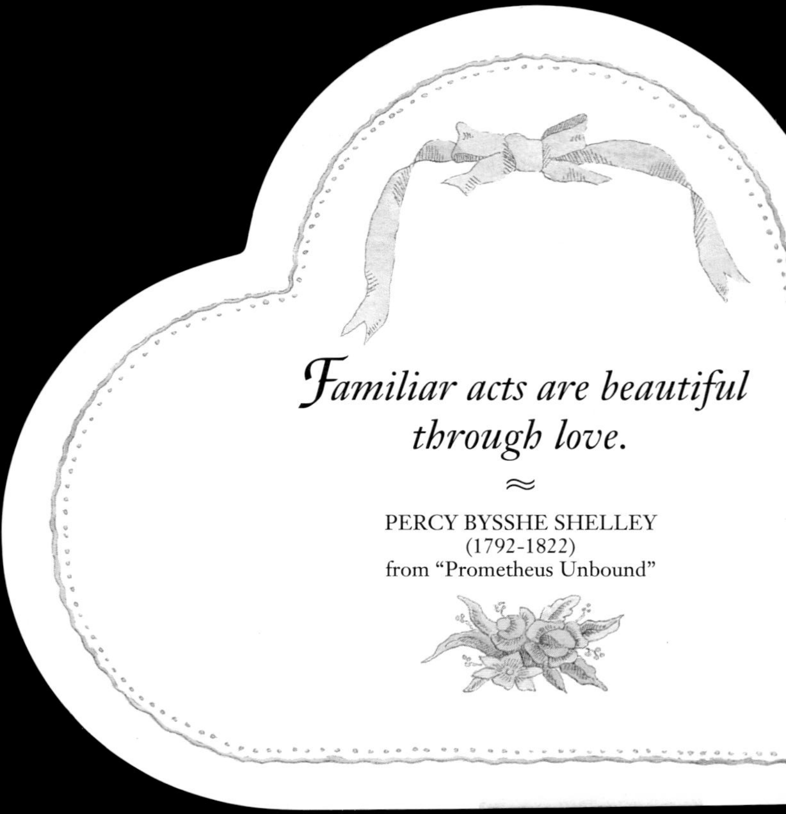
Familiar acts are beautiful
through love.
≈
PERCY BYSSHE SHELLEY
(1792-1822)
from "Prometheus Unbound"

The sweetest joy, the wildest woe is love.

≈

P. J. BAILEY
(1816-1902)
from "Festus: A Love and Garden"

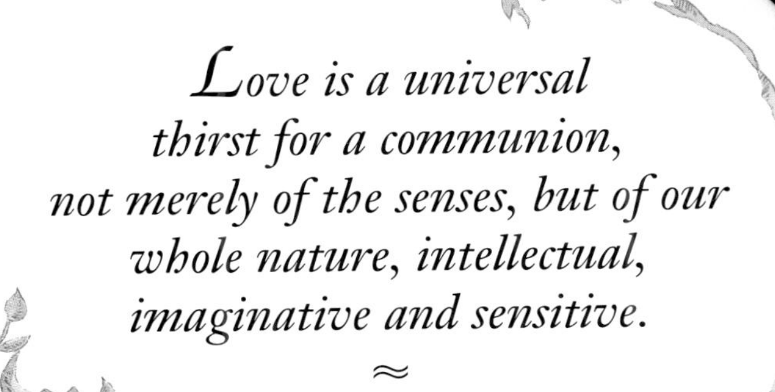

Love is a universal
thirst for a communion,
not merely of the senses, but of our
whole nature, intellectual,
imaginative and sensitive.

≈

BENJAMIN DISRAELI
(1804-1881)

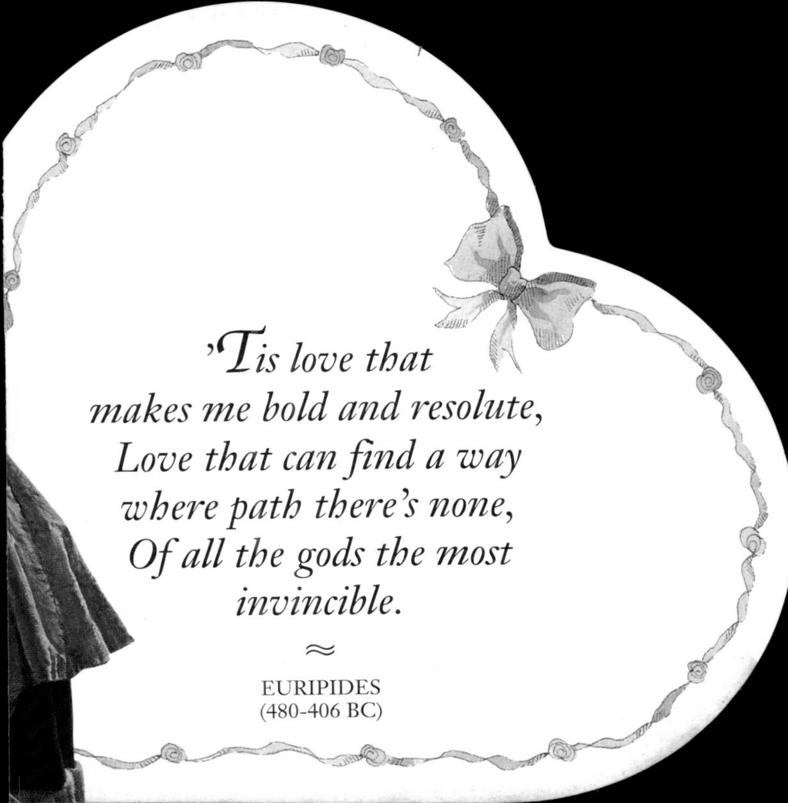

'Tis love that
makes me bold and resolute,
Love that can find a way
where path there's none,
Of all the gods the most
invincible.

≈

EURIPIDES
(480-406 BC)

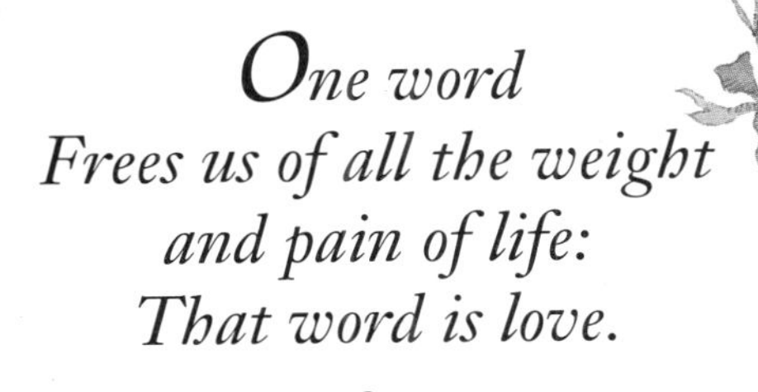

One word
Frees us of all the weight
and pain of life:
That word is love.

≈

SOPHOCLES
(496-406 BC)
from "Oedipus at Colonus"

Love is like a rose, the
joy of all the earth...
Love is like a lovely rose, the
world's delight.
CHRISTINA ROSSETTI
(1830-1874)
from "Hope" in "Collected Poems"

O love is the crooked thing,
There is nobody wise enough
To find out all that is in it,
For he would be thinking of love
Till the stars had run away
And the shadows eaten the moon....

≈

W. B. YEATS
(1865-1939)